Valencia and

A glance at African Spain

Albert Frederick Calvert

Alpha Editions

This edition published in 2024

ISBN : 9789362098566

Design and Setting By
Alpha Editions
www.alphaedis.com
Email - info@alphaedis.com

As per information held with us this book is in Public Domain.
This book is a reproduction of an important historical work. Alpha Editions uses the best technology to reproduce historical work in the same manner it was first published to preserve its original nature. Any marks or number seen are left intentionally to preserve its true form.

Contents

THE OLD KINGDOM OF VALENCIA .... - 1 -
SAGUNTUM AND CASTELLON .... - 12 -
THE KINGDOM OF MURCIA .... - 15 -

THE OLD KINGDOM OF VALENCIA

SHUT in between the barren range of the Sierra Molina on the north, and the arid plains of Murcia to the south, the ancient Kingdom of Valencia is one of the regions of Spain least visited by the tourist. And yet, a flowering and fruitful Eden, it lies beneath a burning sun, its waters trained in obedience to the hand of man. It puts forth a vegetation of tropical luxuriance. Demeter has blessed the land. Under the soft caressing winds that sweep up from the Mediterranean the soil yields four or five crops in the year to the industry of the peasant. And if at times the dreaded sirocco, charged with poisonous vapours from the Albufera, lays the country prostrate—well, for every Paradise was devised a snake!

The people of the province, with the exception of those of Orihuela, speak that variety of the Romance which I may call Catalan, and which, with local modification, is common all along the eastern coast of Spain from the mouth of the Segura to the frontier of Rousillon. Limousin, as it is sometimes called, is not a mere dialect, but a quite distinct language, a survival of the old *Langue d'oc*. Probably it was spoken by those Romanised Spaniards who were driven north of the Pyrenees by the Arabic invasion. It would be restored by them when they reconquered this portion of their old territory. The Christian population, before Valencia was recovered by Jaime el Conqueridor of Aragon, spoke Castilian or a tongue akin to it. But the Catalan of the new rulers was stronger, and soon swept aside the common speech of the people. Curiously enough, this same Catalan was not the language used in Aragon itself, a fact which no doubt had a strong determining influence in the choice of Castilian at the time of the unification of the two kingdoms. Why Orihuela alone clung to its old Castilian tongue in despite of the Conqueror is not clear, unless it was owing merely to the proximity of Murcia.

In character the Valencians are superstitious, revengeful, relentless in hate. "Ni olvido ni perdono" is their motto. They love the colour and joy of life. Dancing and love-making are their chief delights. And yet they are a laborious race. But their white, rather flabby appearance proclaims them lacking in backbone and initiative. "Flesh is grass, and grass is water. The men are women, the women—nothing!" says their own proverb.

The fertile huerta has found its novelist in Blasco Ibañez, a native of Valencia, who has beautifully described the languid life of the province. A translation must necessarily lack the force and elegance of the master's style, but the following passages will at least enable the reader to picture a summer in the south:

"When the vast plain awakes in the bluish light of dawn, the last of the nightingales that have sung through the night breaks off abruptly in his final trill, as though he had been stricken by the steely shaft of day. Sparrows in whole coveys burst forth from the thatched roofs, and beneath this aerial rabble preening their wings the trees shake and nod.

"One by one the murmurs of the night subside; the trickling of the water-courses, the sighing of the reeds, the barking of the watchful dogs, other sounds belonging to the day, grow louder and fill the huerta, the crow of the cock is heard from every farm, and the village bells proclaim the call to prayer borne across from the towers of Valencia, which are yet misty in the distance. From the farmyards arises a discordant animal concert—the neighing of horses, the bellowing of oxen, the clucking of hens, the bleating of lambs, the grunting of swine—the sounds produced by beasts that scent the keen odour of vegetation in the morning breeze and are hungry for the fields.

"The sky is suffused with light, and with light life inundates the plain and penetrates to the interior of human and animal abodes. Doors open creaking. In the porches white figures appear, their hands clasped behind their necks, scanning the horizon. From the stables issue towards the city milch cows, herds of goats, manure-carts. Bells tinkle between the dwarf trees bordering the high road, and every now and again is heard the sharp "Arre, Aca" of the drivers.

"On the thresholds of the cottages those bound for the town exchange greetings with those who stay in the fields. 'Bon dia nos done Deu!' [May God give us a good day!] 'Bon Dia.'

"Immense is the energy, the explosion of life at midsummer, the best season of the year, the time of harvest and abundance. Space throbs with light and heat. The African sun rains torrents of fire on the land already crackled and wrinkled by its burning caresses, and its golden beams pierce the dense foliage, beneath which are hidden the canals and trenches to save them from the all-powerful vivifying heat.

"The branches of the trees are heavy with fruit. They bend beneath the weight of yellow grapes covered with glazed leaves. Like the pink cheeks of a child grow the apricots amid the verdure. Children greedily eye the luxurious burden of the fig-trees. From the gardens is wafted the scent of jasmin, and the magnolias dispense their incense in the burning air, laden with the perfume of cereals.

"The gleaming scythe has already sheared the land, levelling the golden fields of wheat and the tall corn-stalks which bowed beneath their heavy load of life. The hay forms yellow hills which reflect the colour of the sun. The wheat is winnowed in a whirlwind of dust; in the naked fields among the stubble sparrows hop from spot to spot in search of stray gleanings. Everywhere are happiness and joyous labour. Waggons go groaning down the road; children frolic in the fields and among the sheaves, thinking of the wheaten cakes in prospect, and of the lazy pleasant life which begins for the farmer when his barn is filled. Even the old horses stride along more gaily, cheered by the smell of the golden grain which will flow steadily into their mangers as the year rolls on.

"When the harvest has levelled the panorama and cleared the great stretches of wheat sprinkled with poppies, the plain seems vast, almost illimitable. Farther than the eye can reach stretch its great squares of red soil, marked off by paths and trenches. The Sunday's rest is rigorously observed over the whole countryside. Not a man is seen toiling in the fields, not a beast at work on the road. Down the paths pass old women with their mantillas drawn over their eyes, and their little chairs hanging to their arms. In the distance resound, like the tearing of linen, the shots fired at the swallows, which fly hither and thither in circles. A noise seems to be produced by their wings ruffling the crystal firmament. From the canals rises the murmur of clouds of almost invisible flies. In a farm all painted blue, under an ancient arbour, there is a whirlwind of gaily-coloured shawls and petticoats, while the guitars with their drowsy rhythm and the strident cornets accompany the measures of the Valencian 'Jota.'

"In the village the little plaza is thronged with the field-folk. The men are in their shirt-sleeves with black sashes and gorgeous handkerchiefs arranged mitre-like on their heads. The old men lean on their big Liria sticks. The young men, with sleeves turned up, display their red nervous arms and carry mere sprigs of ash between their huge knotted fingers.

"In the afternoon, towards the fountain along the road, bordered with poplars which shake their silvered foliage, go groups of girls with their pitchers on their heads. Their rhythmical movements and their grace recall the Athenian Canephori. This procession to the well lends to the huerta something of a Biblical character. The Fontana de la Reina is the pride of the huerta, condemned to drink the water of wells, and the red and dirty liquid of the canals. It is esteemed as an ancient and valuable work. It has a square basin with walls of reddish stone. The water is below the soil. You reach the bottom by means of six green and slippery steps. Opposite the steps is a defaced bas-relief, probably a Virgin attended by angels—no doubt an ex-voto of the time of the Conquest. Laughter and chatter are not wanting round the well. The girls cluster round, eager to fill their pitchers but in no hurry to depart. They jostle each other on the steps, with their petticoats gathered in between their legs, the better to lean forward and to plunge their vessels into the basin. The surface of the water is unceasingly troubled by the bubbles rising from the sandy bed, which is covered with weeds waving in the current."

The exuberant natural life pictured in these passages is not altogether due to the bounty of nature. The scorching sun would have brought death instead of life to Valencia without the co-operation of man. The whole province is a triumph of irrigation. The Moors were masters of hydraulic science. They tapped the Jucar and the Guadalaviar and drew their waters through the Moncada and seven smaller but magnificent canals into every corner of the land. This was the legacy they left behind when they were so suicidally expelled. Their successors, as Mr. Richard Ford so eloquently puts it, exercise "a magic control over water, wielding it at their bidding"—presumably as Gilbert's hero Ferdinando brandished the turtle soup!

Bequeathed also directly by the Moors, the Tribunal of the Waters is the most interesting sight of Valencia. It is independent of all law; no Government has ever touched it; it has no written records. The court meets every Thursday morning at eleven o'clock at the Apostles' Gate of the Cathedral in the capital, to try all cases and disputes in regard to the precious water that is the life-blood of the province. There are seven judges, one for each canal, elected by the peasantry of the districts, and each is known by the name of his canal—Mislata, Cuarte, and so forth. They are grave, stoutly-built men, with tanned faces and close-cropped hair. They wear black, the colour beloved by the comfortably situated working man all the world over; but they have not degenerated quite so far as to discard the native handkerchief round their polished brows, or the espadrilla, the Valencian shoe.

Except that the turban has given place to the sombrero and the divan to an ancient sofa, the proceedings of the tribunal are as patriarchal as of old. In the plaza a crowd of litigants are collected, chattering, gesticulating, arguing their wrongs according to the manner of their kind all the world over. With an air of importance befitting the occasion the Alguazil of the tribunal places the magisterial bench in the shadow of the great Gothic portal. A light rail will keep the vulgar at a distance. Then the peasant magistrates take their seats, and the oldest pronounces the words, "Se abri el tribunal" (The tribunal is open). A portentous silence falls, for any one who speaks before his turn must pay a fine. One by one the litigants are introduced within the railing and plead their cause bareheaded before the court. Woe to the insolent wight that dare stand covered in its presence. The Alguazil will tear the handkerchief from off his head, and he will also be mulcted in a fine. Each must await the tapping of the presidential foot before he ventures into the presence. But the severity of the discipline does not suffice to make the fiery Valencians restrain their feelings. At every moment there is an explosion of wrath or indignation, a heated expostulation from one or other of the parties. The fines collected must be a considerable sum. Out of their own wisdom the judges give their decisions, which are almost invariably received without discontent. The Valencians are anxious to preserve their unique tribunal from criticism and interference, for they know that in Spain, as in other countries, royal justice is a costly matter.

The history of Valencia for all practical purposes is that of its capital and namesake. "Its name," says Mr. Ford, "is fondly derived from, or considered equivalent to, Roman, because Ρώμη in Greek signifies power, as Valencia does in Latin." The principle is doubtless excellent, but seems to be that of *lucus a non lucendo*.

When the warriors of Viriathus surrendered to Rome on the death of their chief, Valencia was granted to them by the Consul D. Junius Brutus. Destroyed by Pompey, it became a *colonia* when rebuilt and the capital of the Edetani. But the history of few Roman colonies, as it has reached us, is of interest. The province had the usual martyrs under the persecution of Diocletian and Decius, and was the place of banishment of the zealot Ermengild. Proud of its haughty name, Valencia has yet allowed itself to be taken and retaken oftener than any other city in the world. In 413 it yielded to the Goths, and three hundred years later with great nonchalance transferred its allegiance to the Moor. It formed at one time part of the Khalifate; and again, one or more petty kingdoms in itself.

Don Feodoro Lleorente speaks of "the slave kings" of Valencia. It is certain that many of its rulers were slave adventurers from the palace of the Khalifa, who, like the janizaries of Turkey had literally carved their fortunes with their swords. One of these princes added the Balearic Isles to his realms and unsuccessfully attempted the conquest of Sardinia.

The kingdom thus founded by military adventurers was overthrown by the most famous of that warlike brood.

The Moors had made the desert blossom like the rose. Wealth and prosperity had been secured to the province. The Moslem paradise was located here. Medinat-u-Tarab was its capital—the City of Mirth. The greedy eyes of Christian neighbours were inevitably drawn to such a region, and the break-up of the Ummeyah dynasty offered an excellent opportunity for interference.

Valencia was split up into factions, and the King or Amir Kadir was merely the puppet of the two opposing parties, who alternately supported him on his tottering throne. But the Moors were a proud race and felt themselves dishonoured in yielding homage to so weak a ruler. Headed by Ibn Jahhaf, the people rose in revolt. Kadir fled, but was detected under his woman's disguise, was taken and beheaded. That strange anomaly a Mohammedan republic was formed. A council of the leaders was constituted with Ibn Jahhaf as President.

A people which arrogates the right to choose its ruler has ever been considered a sort of pirate among the nations, and fair game for more powerful States. Kadir, at the time of his deposition, had been under the hardly disinterested protection of the Cid, who, under pretence of avenging his *protégé's* death, immediately advanced on Valencia. For some time Ibn Jahhaf, who seems to have had some of the qualities of a great general, amused the Campeador with negotiations, while he pushed hastily forward preparations for defence. Discovering that he was being played with, the Cid swept through the country and threw his army round Valencia, which for twenty months made a stubborn resistance. The city falling at length, Jahhaf, who had become a special object of hatred to the Conqueror, was burnt alive in the plaza. Until his death in 1097, the Cid ruled the kingdom as absolute lord and despot. The legend runs that Ximena, his wife, defended the city for two years after her husband's death. And so great was the reputation and the terror of the Campeador that she finally won a victory over the Mussulmans and carried him to his last resting-place at Cardeña by the stratagem of placing his corpse fully armed upon his war-horse with his celebrated sword in his hand.

But for two centuries longer Valencia followed the law of the Prophet. It was finally wrested from the yoke of Islam on the memorable 28th of September 1238, when the standard of the victorious Jaime I. of Aragon was hoisted over the tower of Ali Bufat, and the Crescent bowed before the Cross. The conquest in the history of Aragon ranks with the taking of Seville in the history of Castile. Granada was the joint conquest of both kingdoms. The way in which the Moors in these old days surrendered their whole kingdom to the Christians, sometimes after only one battle had been fought, stands out in dark contrast with the tenacious resistance offered by their descendants in Algeria in modern times. Enervated by the climate of Spain the Mussulmans of that country were absolutely incapable of maintaining a prolonged guerilla warfare. If a fortified capital was taken they at once handed over the whole kingdom to the conqueror. They were not of course peculiar in this respect. The sentiments of nationality and physical courage are characteristic far more of the modern than of the ancient world. We have only to compare the resistance of the Anglo-Saxons to the Normans with that of the Boers to the British, of the French in the Hundred Years War with that of their descendants in 1871, to realise how much more of manliness and endurance we possess than did our ancestors. We must go back to the days of Leonidas and Regulus to find parallels for the exploits of our own Indian Army; to Numantia and Seguntum for parallels to Saragossa and Gerona. National and individual self-respect withered under feudalism, and revived only on the introduction of free institutions.

The commerce and wealth of the country now fell into the hands of the Jews, who came over in great numbers from Aragon. For a long time the industrious people lived, hated it is true, but unmolested, in their own quarter of the city. But one ill-fated day a band of children, urged on probably by some fanatic, marched against the Jewry crying that they had come to baptize the unbelieving dogs, and that the Archdeacon of Seville was close upon their heels. In terror the wretched people retreated to their homes, firmly barricading themselves. Some of the Christian children got shut up in the quarter. Like wildfire the rumour spread through the streets that the Jews were submitting them to untold tortures behind their barred doors. The whole populace went mad with the rage for blood, attacked the wholly unprepared Jews, and the most horrible scenes of massacre ensued. This was in 1391. The prosperity of Valencia suffered its first severe blow with the barbarous expulsion of the Moors at the command of Philip III. Another fell some time later when, on account of its strenuous opposition to the French claim to the Crown, Philip V. confiscated the liberties of the province and imposed an enormous fine.

But Valencia, though fallen from its old estate, is nevertheless to-day a thriving prosperous province; its capital is handsome and progressive. Busy life pulsates through the streets; the *cafés* are alive with the hum of voices. There is little to recall the days of its allegiance to the Prophet, and it has not retained more monuments of the past than most other cities. From the sightseer's point of view it is not intensely interesting; from the stranger's, even less convenient, since indications of the names of the streets are few and far between. New and splendid avenues are arising, which, in pleasant contrast to the dull uniformity of most Continental town perspectives, contain houses original and individual in style. You enter the town by one of two massive castellated gates, which give a note of the mediæval picturesque to their respective quarters. The fourteenth century Torres de Serranos form a narrow archway flanked by two fine octagonal towers. Above, are windows with elaborate panelling, and heavy machicolations crown the whole building. The Torres de Cuartes, of a century later, are very similar, but the parapet is itself borne on corbels and machicolated. Unfortunately the walls of the city have perished.

The Cathedral, the Lonja, and the Picture Gallery exhaust the sights of Valencia. The Cathedral was founded in 1262 on the ruins of the Great Mosque, which in its turn had replaced the Temple of Diana. It is far inferior to most of the great Spanish churches in beauty and interest. Originally Gothic, it was considerably enlarged in the fifteenth century, the height, however, being left unaltered. The principal entrance, in the receding circular form, is an outrage, but the north door, called the Puerta de los Apostoles, richly sculptured and delicately moulded, exhibits the skill and industry of the fourteenth century at its best.

Above the semicircular Puerta de Palau is an interesting series of medallions. These represent the heads of fourteen men and women. These are the seven knights of the Conquest and the seven fair ladies they sought in the surrounding provinces, from whom the whole Valencian nobility is said to be sprung. This doorway is evidently by the same hand as the Puerta de los Infantes at Lerida. But the most striking part of the Cathedral is the imposing Miguelete Tower. Its sculpture is indifferent, but seen from a distance the effect is fine. It is the great landmark of the district, and the Valencians speak of exile as "losing sight of the Miguelete."

The plan of the Cathedral, like most Spanish churches, is cruciform. In 1760 the interior was modernised in a manner that makes the beauty-loving traveller long to tear his hair—or that of the perpetrator of the "restoration." Over-decoration is its chief defect. The walls have been encrusted with marbles, the Gothic columns almost concealed by Corinthian pilasters, the pointed arches rounded off. The church may merit its surname of "La Rica," but it has lost that atmosphere of remote beauty that calls forth the instincts of religion in the worshipper. During the French occupation of 1809 the magnificent silver altar was melted down, but fortunately its protecting door panels were uninjured. These are painted with six pictures by Francisco Pagano and Pablo de San Leocadio, disciples of Leonardo da Vinci, and ascribed by some to the master himself. The spurs and bridle of Jaime el Conqueridor, presented by him on the day he took the city to his Master of the Horse, are preserved on one of the pillars on the Gospel side.

The choir is for the most part modern, with plain and classical walnut stalls. The rear portion, or *trascoro*, dates from the fifteenth century, and is decorated with a fine series of Biblical scenes in alabaster. The chapels have little of interest, except the tomb of Tomás de Villanueva, the holy Archbishop of Valencia, in the one dedicated to him. Over the crossing rises the fine octagonal lantern, which was built in 1404 and restored in 1731. It was once adorned by many trophies, among them the flags taken from the Genoese by Ramon Corveran, a famous sea-dog of Valencia. These, however, have long since vanished.

After the Cathedral the Lonja de la Seda, or Silk Exchange, is the most interesting sight of Valencia. Built in the Gothic style (though not of the purest) it is one of the best specimens of civil architecture of the Middle Ages that we have remaining. Its square tower, crenellated chimneys, open galleries and high windows give an extremely fine effect. The hall has spirally fluted pillars that branch out into graceful clusters of palm-leaves. The ceiling is painted with stars and round the walls runs the legend, "He only that shall not have deceived nor done usury shall be worthy of eternal life," which (let us hope) has guided generations of merchants into the paths of commercial integrity. The Audiencia, in good Renaissance style, is well worth a visit, where in the Salon de Cortes the old provincial States assembled till the middle of the eighteenth century. As a building the University is beautiful, if it is a little backward in thought. Here Fernando VII. raised the noble sport of *Tauromachy*, or Bull-fighting, to the dignity of a Faculty!

The smaller churches are interesting enough, but not striking, and the visitor will do well to prefer the almost deserted Picture Gallery. Until the name of Velasquez dwarfed that of every other Spanish artist, Valencia boasted a school of painting second to none in the country. Ribalta, Juanes, Ribera, Espinosa, and Orrente all lived and loved and painted in the old kingdom. The story of Ribalta is romantic. The son of a ploughman, he deemed himself on the high road to fortune when he entered a Valencian studio as a pupil. But alas! the black eyes and pretty figure of his master's daughter proved more alluring than canvas virgins. Ribalta was dismissed the studio in disgrace. He wandered towards Italy, the land of promise, and studied under the brothers Carracci. Some years later he returned. His mistress was in possession of the studio, her father having gone out. A wooden and lifeless Madonna stood on an easel. Ribalta seized a brush and painted furiously until sunset, and when the artist returned a masterpiece was awaiting him. Astonishment, admiration, tears, and gratitude—no artist could forbid his daughter's *fiançailles* with a man of genius. Ribalta afterwards devoted his whole life to the adornment of the churches of his native kingdom.

But Valencia is hardly less distinguished for its theatre than for its painting. Here at the end of the sixteenth century was founded the celebrated society of "Nocturnes" which welcomed the youth of Lope de Vega. Guillen de Castro was its head, a man of wit and honourable family, whose adventurous life ended in the gutter. He is best known as the author of *Las Mocedades del Cid*, a tedious drama with a fine heroic touch, whence Corneille drew his inspiration.

Leaving Valencia we run southward as far as Alcira without a stop. Here we cross the Jucar, which strikes terror into the hearts of the townsfolk. Rising in the rainy season with terrible rapidity, with constant shiftings of its channel, it sweeps over the countryside, swallowing up whole villages in its destructive, impetuous course. When the sky grows black and the river starts to rise, the panic-stricken inhabitants run to the churches and seize the images. Then with frenzied prayers to the *Pare San Bernard*, they dip the holy forehead in the water, hoping to stay the onrush of the torrent. But the inundated country to-day will in a few years bear heavy rice crops and luxuriant orchards. The swampy unhealthy lagoon, the Albufera (which gave its name to one of Napoleon's marshals) is becoming filled up with the *débris* brought down from the mountains. Soon it, too, will be a fertile huerta. Meanwhile, trees are being planted on the rugged hill-side, a wise measure which it is hoped will check the violence of the floods and the denudation of the arid soil.

Jativa will be our next stopping-place. Like most of the towns in this country it is rich in historic interest. Past cottages, embosomed in palm-and orange-trees, you climb up to the hill where the old and new castles stand side by side. Here in 1284 the Infantes de la Cerda, rightful heirs to the throne, were confined by their Uncle Sancho el Bravo. Here too the Duke of Calabria, heir of Naples, languished for ten years after having trusted himself to the honour of Gonzalo de Cordoba, who betrayed him. This was one of the three deeds of which Gonzalo is said to have repented at the last. Indeed the castle of Jativa seems to have greatly troubled his death-bed, for we learn that the second of these three misdeeds was the imprisonment in the same place of the infamous Cæsar Borgia. The Borgias—those super-men of the Renaissance—had their origin in the neighbourhood of Jativa, which also boasts itself the birthplace of the artist Ribera.

The smaller coast towns of Alicante attract the weary traveller by their beautifully sounding names: Benidorm, Villajoyosa—what pleasant chords they strike in the imagination! But time is short. You think of them regretfully and hurry towards the capital. But first, if the month is April, you must turn aside for a flying visit to Alcoy, where every year a mediæval joust takes place to the glory of Saint George (the city's patron saint) and the discomfiture of the Moors. This is to celebrate the taking of the town from the Moors by Jaime el Conqueridor in 1253.

Alicante, the largest town in the province of that name, and the second in the Kingdom of Valencia, is as dull as most thriving commercial centres. Its broad white quays are thronged with a busy bustling humanity. Touches of vivid colour in the dress of the women, who are labouring like navvies, a burning sun overhead, and the blue of the Mediterranean, make a not unpleasing picture. Behind the town towers an enormous rock—a second Gibraltar—crowned by the old castle of Santa Barbara. A deep fissure in the rock recalls the stubborn siege of 1707, when the English General and all his garrison were blown to pieces by a mine.

Southwards still, to Elche, the City of Palms, or, less poetically, "The Frying-pan!" A mist of heat seems to hang over the little Oriental-looking town. Not even in the palm groves that shut out the desert can you avoid it. These magnificent trees (it has been estimated that there are 80,000 in the belt that encircles the town) provide practically all the palms used by the Christian churches in Passion Week. In the shade of their avenues flourish the laurel, the rose, and the geranium; beyond, extend crops of lucerne and wheat, watered by the carefully regulated Vinalapo.

But though Elche makes an agreeable impression on travellers, in Spain it is chiefly celebrated for its Passion or Mystery Play, the only one of its kind in the kingdom. Elche is under the special protection of Our Lady of the Assumption, who sent her miraculous image over the seas along with the words and music of the opera inscribed *Soy para Elche* (I am for Elche). To this image, supposed to have been found in 1370 by a coastguard named Canto, many houses and palm plantations round the city belong. They are all marked with a crown and the initials M.V. The image is said to have been carved by St. Luke, but hardly reflects credit on his skill. However, the miracles it performs seem highly satisfactory, judging by the magnificent jewels and garments that have been presented by the faithful.

The opera is presented on August 13 and 14, the eve and the feast of the Assumption. In a country where the sister of Cervantes was allowed to install a theatre in her convent and herself play the leading *rôles*, you are not surprised to find that the representation takes place in the church, which is, however, for the occasion, carefully stripped of sacred images.

The scenery, as in mediæval days, is simple. There is a little cave for the Garden of Gethsemane, a plain coffin for the Holy Sepulchre. Angels playing harps on a blue cloth stretched across the roof betoken the celestial regions. Hence, by an ingenious arrangement of ropes and pulleys, angels will presently come down to take the Virgin up to heaven. Apostles and saints, their names legibly inscribed on cardboard haloes, the holy angels and the Trinity itself have all their appointed parts. The Virgin is a small boy of eleven. Unfortunately that touch of vulgarity which seems inseparable from modern Continental Catholicism liberally decorates the angels with well-greased hair, vivid sashes, and paper flowers of startling hues. However, the crowded audience is not critical and very real emotion at times interrupts the continuous chatter and shaking of fans. There seems something singularly human in a religion so all-embracing.

Orihuela, in its fertile plain, rendered independent of rain by the waters of the Segura, will be our last stopping-place in the southern portion of the kingdom. Here the Goths made a last resistance under Theodomir. Orihuela is the only city in the district where Castilian is spoken. Its square towers and domes shaded with palms are decidedly Oriental in appearance. A visit to the Cathedral shows some beautiful choir-stalls of carved mahogany, but the interior of the building has been hopelessly barbarised. There is little else to detain us here, so we take train again for Valencia and the north.

SAGUNTUM AND CASTELLON

LEAVING the city of Valencia, the traveller journeys northwards through one of the most luxuriant garden-plains of southern Europe. Groves of olive, almond, and orange trees crowd thick upon each other, their almost monotonous fruitfulness broken only by an occasional graceful cluster of stately palms. Soon there comes in sight a hill crowned with an irregular line of battlemented walls. Its silhouette is warm against the sky-line. This is Saguntum, famed in story.

You pass out of the station and on your left rise up the eastern slopes of the Saguntine hill. At its feet are huddled the dark green tiled roofs of the village, from among which the little church of San Salvador detaches its quadrangular tower, proudly conscious that (in the eye of its worshippers at least) it is the oldest Christian foundation in the whole of Spain. Tiny cottages gleam white in the dark places of the rocks, between thickets of aloes and prickly-pear. And far above, the reddish walls of the castle with its huge square towers stretch in slanting belts along the summit of the hill, keeping watch over the ever-retreating sea that has so often been studded with the ships of enemies.

To the right, coaches from Teruel and Segorbe lumber along a white ribbon of road, smothered in clouds of dust. Clambering up the fence of masonry that separates populace and passengers a dozen Saguntine youths, burnt by the sun, with eyes like sloes and jet-black hair, hail you in eager tones. They thrust towards you sinewy arms holding cups of milk or wine and plates of savoury meats, with branches of oranges or wands garlanded with fruits and sweet-smelling flowers.

But it is a silent town, Saguntum (or Murviedro as it is generally called), and seems to brood on memories of the past. Founded in 1389 B.C. by the Greeks of Zacynthus, it has been held in turn by Carthaginian and Roman, by Goth, Moor, and Spaniard. Its place in history is unique. The story of its famous siege has repeatedly been told.

It is the year 219 B.C.—the eve of the Second Punic War. Hannibal, having sworn war to the death on Rome, is gathering his forces for a crushing blow. The wealth of Saguntum attracts him; impoverished by the loss of Sicily, its position as frontier town appeals to him as a strategist; as the ally of Rome it draws his hatred. Suddenly a force of a hundred and fifty thousand Carthaginian soldiers is hurled against the town; battering-rams thunder at the gates; huge catapults scatter death among the startled townsfolk. Then begins a struggle that can be compared only with Numantia in ancient or Saragossa in modern times. Force and cunning have met their match in desperate heroism.

The siege lasted for eight months. Rome was appealed to, but her Ambassadors were not allowed to land. They turned to Carthage and entered the Senate House. "I bring you peace or war," cried Valerius Flaccus; "choose which you will have!" and resounding cries of "War! War!" initiated one of the fiercest struggles of antiquity. But though fighting against a common enemy, Rome deserted her Spanish ally.

A city beseiged is a city doomed. Saguntum could hold out no longer. Hannibal named his terms—life and two garments to each individual. Arms, wealth, and Fatherland must all be given up, and the inhabitants must drift to whatever part of the world the conqueror decreed.

Immediately, by order of the Senate, a scaffold was erected in the public square. All the wealth from the public treasury was flung upon it. Private citizens added their treasures to the holocaust, and with the courage of despair flung themselves into the flames. Then a shout arose from the walls; one of the towers had fallen and the attacking army swarmed over the ramparts to wholesale massacre. Such is Livy's account, but it is probably an overstatement. For though the Carthaginians, being a Semitic race, were capable of any cruelty, history records that the first act of the Scipios, on rebuilding the town four years later, was to buy back the exiled inhabitants.

Two thousand years later Saguntum was once again the theatre of war, when in 1808 it was attacked and taken by Marshal Suchet. But Napoleon's success was as ephemeral as Hannibal's. The French violet could not take root in the granite of Spain.

The present castle is principally Moorish, though some traces of the old Saguntine walls can be distinguished. It is probable that the keep described by Livy occupied the site of the present citadel. There are some old Moorish cisterns to which the girls of the village climb in the evening with water-jars on their shoulders.

A little lower down the hill lies the ancient Roman amphitheatre, the most nearly perfect of its kind that exists to-day, not even excepting those of Italy. The separate entrances that Roman ceremony required for knights and magistrates, for women and for the common people, can still be recognised in spite of the depredations of Suchet and the Philistines. Its thirty-three tiers of bluish grey pebbles, cemented cunningly together to look like huge blocks of stone, rise with the sloping hill-side. The theatregoer of Murviedro had little to complain of in the old days. If the play was tedious, he could turn his eye to the beautiful scenery that lay before him. His lot was enviable beside the Londoner's.

The plain that now separates Murviedro from the sea is rich in ruins of a bygone age. Desultory excavations have yielded some results. In 1795 a magnificent mosaic was discovered representing Bacchus astride a tiger in the midst of revellers, which, unfortunately, has since been lost. For the antiquary with money at his back and method in his brain a rich and interesting harvest lies waiting.

Leaving Saguntum we continue northwards past the picturesque old castle of Almenara; past Nules, famous for its mineral springs; past Burriana, whose oranges you have eaten in every country of Europe; and the train steams at length into Castellon de la Plana. To the eye this city is uninteresting enough, but the imagination is touched by the recital of its history.

A league to the north of the town the barren mountains of the Desierta rise from an arid plain. Here can be seen some crumbling grey walls and a hermitage in honour of St. Mary Magdalena. The walls mark the site of the old town captured in 1233 by Jaime I. of Aragon. A few years later the inhabitants petitioned the King's lieutenant for leave to remove their town to the fertile plain on the coast where it now stands. Not only was this granted but considerable privileges were bestowed on the enterprising city.

Every year on the third Sunday in Lent this event is commemorated by the Feast of Las Gayates. Clergy and laity alike, bearing green reeds, proceed in pilgrimage to the hermitage, where a solemn service is celebrated. A gay crowd invades the hill. They sing; they dance; they shout; they eat and drink. After this sylvan feast, they troop back to the town. At nightfall a second procession sets out, in which are represented with all edifying accompaniments the worldly pomps and repentance of the Magdalene. Raised up among a myriad flashing lanterns the "Gayata," which gives its name to the festival and recalls the removal of the city, is borne along with song and dance.

More than once has Castellon fought bravely in defence of its liberties. A very strenuous resistance was offered to Pedro IV. when the women fought side by side with the men upon the walls. One of the amazon warriors killed a relative of the attacking General, Don Pedro de Boil, and was hanged in the market-place on the fall of the city, along with the other rebel leaders. Considering the part that Spanish women have played in the history of their country, it is curious to remember that voluptuous indolence is supposed to entirely sum up their character. The War of the Brotherhood, that great popular rising, gave three more martyrs to Castellon. It is not, therefore, surprising to find that this city to-day stands, in the province to which it gives its name, for democratic tendencies. So Morella on its rocky throne, the stronghold of the ferocious Carlist chief, Cabrera, stands for aristocratic militarism; and Segorbe, lying in the shadow of the magnificent monastery of Valdecristo, for the ecclesiastical element and clerical control.

THE KINGDOM OF MURCIA

THE ancient Kingdom of Murcia, which lies to the south of Valencia, includes the two modern provinces of Murcia and Albacete. It is a wild, fierce region, where the sun's heat scorches all vegetation from off the hill-sides. Deep and terrible chasms yawn between the rugged mountains; there are sharp and rocky peaks that seem to have been thrown up by sudden upheavals of the earth, and at their feet lie great stretches of tawny desert recalling the burning expanse of the Sahara. The shadow of long-continued drought often broods over the whole kingdom. But yet the district watered by the Segura is an earthly paradise—in spring all flowers, in autumn all fruit. Mingling with the carob-tree and broad-leaved palm glistens the gold of oranges, and luxuriant vines give pleasant promise of a sparkling harvest.

But nature has not thus blessed the land of her own free will. She needed coaxing and much wooing by the cunning Arabs. A wonderful system of irrigation prevails, and science has harnessed fast the wayward rivers. The greatest treasure of the Murcian, water, is sold by auction to the highest bidder. M. Jean Brunhés, in a lately published work, gives some very curious and interesting details relating to this singular system.

The volume of the Monegre is divided into old and new water, the former belonging of right to the ancient riparian proprietors, the latter to the owners of the locks and reservoirs. A very vicious system prevails at Lorca. There, a private company has obtained all rights in the water of Guadalentin, subject to the condition of supplying the old proprietors of the adjoining lands with 500 litres per second every day. Only in rainy seasons, when the company's barrage is swept away by the torrent (as it usually is some five or six times in the year), does the water become public property. When this happens the company is not allowed to make the barrage any stronger when it is rebuilt. In seasons of drought the owners are masters of the situation, and are able to recoup themselves for the losses thus incurred by forcing up prices to a figure absolutely ruinous to all but the richest cultivators. There is only one palliation to this system, that the bidder who has bought the first lot can buy as many of the lots following as he may desire at the same figure. Notwithstanding this poor concession it would seem that the principle of private ownership has been pushed a little too far in this part of the world.

Here is M. Brunhés' account of the water auction at Lorca:

"The sale takes place in a badly lit hall with naked walls, on a level with the street, with which it communicates by an immense door almost its own breadth. This door remains open during the sale, and the crowd of bidders stand partly in the street. The hall has no floor; you stand on the bare ground. Opposite the door at the end of the hall is a railed-off daïs, entered by a side door, and without any direct communication with the public side. On the daïs the secretaries are seated at a large table covered by a threadbare green cloth. Behind the table are five arm-chairs. In one is seated the presiding officer (a civil engineer who must own no land in the Vega). On a stool is stationed the crier.

"At eight o'clock in the morning, at a sign from the presiding officer, the crier pronounces these words in a singing monotonous voice, and without any pause between the two phrases: 'In honour of the Holy Sacrament of the Altar, who buys the first lot of Sotellana?' Immediately shouts go up, 'Eight, nine, or ten reales!' One voice overpowers the other, wide mouths vociferate loudly, necks are strained, muscles grow tense with excitement. The bidders press and crush each other against the iron railing, for the one nearest has the best chance of being heard. The presiding officer listens and follows the frantic shouting with sovereign calm. Suddenly, with a quick gesture, he designates the highest bidder. At once the clamour ceases. Amid absolute silence the man indicated calls out his name, which the clerks write down.

"The men are hatless. Some wear black or dark-coloured handkerchiefs bound round their heads, but all hold their broad-brimmed hats in their hands. No one smokes or talks till the bidding recommences, and even those in the street are silent and bareheaded. It is easy to see that all are peasants. Heads are closely cropped; here are no beards or moustaches, no one wears a collar, and most carry a cloak other than the aristocratic *capa* on the shoulders or arm. It is a curious and impressive sight enough these bronzed physiognomies, animated by one desire to obtain, as cheaply as may be, possession of the supreme good, water."

Such is the province of Murcia in the twentieth century. When vegetation depended only on the sun and very infrequent rain, the land can have been very little better than an arid wilderness. And yet its possession has from the earliest times been a matter of keen dispute. To the early inhabitants have always been ascribed those simple guileless virtues with which the eighteenth century endowed the noble savage. Like the high-souled inhabitants of More's "Utopia," they used the gold and silver, in which their mountains abounded, for the meanest articles of domestic use. But this admirable custom seems unfortunately to have been based on mere ignorance of the value of their treasures.

More sophisticated were the Phœnicians, who scented the precious metals from afar, and here, as everywhere, established their commercial centres. Next, the Greeks swooped down and planted colonies, rivalry between the two races precipitating the fierce conflict between their respective allies, the Carthaginians and the Romans. New Carthage, or Cartagena, was founded by Hasdrubal; his son made it the starting-place of his famous march to

Rome. The city made a brave resistance to Scipio, and its fall marked the downfall of the Carthaginian in Spain.

As an outpost of the Roman Empire this district was one of the first abandoned to the attacks of the barbarians. Under the Visigoths it became a duchy with the name of Aurariola, which offered so determined a resistance to the Mussulman that it was enabled to retain its independence, subject merely to the Khalifa as suzerain. Here, as in so many Iberian sieges, the women played no small part. Dressed as men, they paraded the walls of the city: and by this stratagem enabled Duke Theodomir to obtain such favourable terms.

Perpetuating the memory of this Duke, the province lasted under the name of Todmir some sixty-eight years as a self-governing State. But the last governors allied themselves with Charlemagne. Arab invaders poured in, who soon swamped the Christian population and Todmir was completely absorbed into the Moslem Empire.

A new capital, Murcia, was founded, that soon rivalled Toledo and Cordoba as a manufactory of arms. After undergoing the usual vicissitudes of Moorish States, it was taken in 1266 by Jaime el Conqueridor, and handed over to his son-in-law, the King of Castile. For two hundred years it endured the attacks of the Moors of Granada, acting meanwhile as a buffer to the Christian kingdom.

Murcia to-day seems a survival of the Middle Ages. The legend goes that Adam returning to earth recognised the province as the only relic of the world he left. The Murcians are a conservative people, clinging to the beliefs and ideas of their forefathers, untouched by the march of thought. Religion is the changeless background of their lives, and often its picturesque ceremonies completely hold the stage. One of the most interesting of their religious festivals is the Passion Procession held on Good Friday. According to tradition this has continued without interruption since 1603, except in the year 1809 only, when it was forbidden by the Government.

Organised by the Confraternity of Jesus, the great feature of the procession is the magnificent series of carved groups (known as *pasos*) representing scenes from the Biblical narrative. These are the work of the great master Salzillo, who is said to have carved no fewer than 1792 wooden figures in his long life of seventy-six years. During the eighteenth century the Trades Guilds of Murcia gave special support to the Confraternity. They are accordingly granted the privilege of carrying the different *pasos* in the procession. Thus the "Kiss of Judas" is borne by the bakers; Santa Veronica by the weavers; while the tailors carry the gigantic group of the Last Supper. The bearers, all alike clad in purple, carry lighted candles and musical instruments. Their hoods shroud their heads, the eyes alone being visible through slits; a knotted rope girdles the waist, and stockings of coarse white wool, instead of the bare feet demanded by the original statute, acknowledge the claims of the twentieth century.

It is six o'clock on Good Friday morning. The streets are thronged with eager sightseers; heads are devoutly bared and many a plain wooden cross is displayed to mark the sympathy of the crowd. A band of mounted gendarmes clears the way. The standard-bearer chants to the populace that "This is done in remembrance of the Passion of Our Lord Jesus Christ." Smothered in flowers the first five *pasos* are borne along. Then to the sound of drum and trumpet, with the ringing of bells and the blare of bugles, Our Father Jesus passes, enveloped in a cloud of flaming candles, accompanied by the Holy Brotherhood. The remaining *pasos* follow close, the clergy and the representatives of King and Bishop bringing up the rear.

The *pasos* themselves will repay inspection. Though abounding in ludicrous anachronisms, often in flabby sentiment, they are beautifully carved and superbly mounted. It is said that £1000 was offered by an enthusiastic German for the uplifted arm of St. Peter in the "Kiss of Judas."

The first group of the Last Supper is of enormous size, requiring no fewer than twenty-four bearers during the procession. Among the tailors of the city there is keen competition for this honour, for the splendid collation that is offered by the pious to the lifeless feasters is later sold by auction for the benefit of the bearers. The price it fetches is no small one, for it is regarded as true *pain béni*, bringing happiness to those who eat. The Agony in the Garden is reputed of supernatural design and is known as "The Pearl of Salzillo." The Angel Gabriel is considered unrivalled, and the legend goes that the Duke of Wellington bid £80,000 for this one figure. The figures are magnificently clothed, the sword and crown of Jesus being set down in the accounts of the brotherhood at £200 and £120 respectively. Perhaps the finest of the groups is that which comes last—our Lady of Dolours, whose expression of supreme sorrow has rarely been equalled whether by chisel or brush. It is said that the sculptor copied it from the countenance of his own daughter, to whom, with this end in view, he had deliberately presented a forged letter announcing the suicide of her betrothed. The *pasos* are deposited in the Ermita de Jesus, where they can be seen by the traveller.

In the town of Murcia itself the influence of the Cross has almost completely banished the Crescent. Gone is the Alcazar, where the Amirs mimicked the State of Cordoba and Toledo; gone is the mosque, where thousands of turbaned heads bowed daily towards Mecca. But in the centre of the city is one of those squares found in every southern and eastern city, which in Spain is always named after the Constitution, in Italy after Victor Emmanuel, and in France after the Republic. To cross it in the afternoon would mean sudden death, for Murcia is one of the hottest corners of Europe. But later a gentle breeze springs up and the citizens troop out to meet with friends upon the Malecon and admire the charming view of the Segura valley, which, as M. Brunhés has said, is "an admirable zone of model agricultural establishment." This fertile huerta bespeaks industry as great as that of the Swiss or Scottish peasant, for the worship of sloth with which Mr. O'Shea charges the Murcian people is groundless and unjust.

A visit to the Cathedral will exhaust the architectural sights of Murcia. Even this is not of first-class interest. Dating in parts from 1386 and Gothic in style, the west front is Churrigueresque, though fortunately not in the most florid style of that unhappy architect. The earthquake of 1829 and a fire in the middle of the last century have greatly damaged the interior, but the general effect is sufficiently striking. The choir-stalls of carved walnut are very beautiful, but the reredos is poor. The eighth wonder of the world, in the opinion of the inhabitants, is the little Velez Chapel modelled on the Constable's Chapel at Burgos, but parts of it, according to Don Rodrigo Amador de los Rios, show the painful caprices and aberrations which announce the death agony of a powerful art. Just beyond the Junteron Chapel, with its wealth of beautifully sculptured figures and designs in the most exuberant Renaissance style, is the urn where the city carefully guards the internal organs of Alfonso the Learned—a gruesome legacy but one greatly valued.

Much older than Murcia, the old Visigothic capital Carthagena has preserved even fewer monuments of antiquity, though it has not lost the military character first impressed upon it by its founder Hasdrubal. For this is the first arsenal of Spain and perhaps its strongest fortress. Its splendid sheltered harbour is defended by powerful forts and formidable batteries. Their fire has not always been directed upon the enemies of Spain. For many months in 1873 over them waved the red flag of the Intransigents, the extreme communistic republicans, who, simultaneously with the Carlists of the north, threatened to ruin Castelar's Government at Madrid. The acquisition of the great national arsenal without firing a shot was, of course, of the utmost advantage to the determined revolutionaries. The garrison, in addition to the enthusiastic population, included several revolted battalions of regular troops under General Contreras.

Against this terrible stronghold of the Revolution, General Martinez Campos advanced with an army from Madrid, with orders to reduce the place with the utmost despatch. This was easier said than done. Supplies were lacking; the advantage in artillery lay entirely with the besieged. The Carlists effected diversions in favour of the Intransigents—an odd coalition. Meanwhile three of the revolutionary vessels were seized by a Prussian squadron as pirates— an utterly unjustifiable interference with the domestic affairs of another State.

The Prussians and Italians exacted, moreover, a war indemnity of 50,000 pesetas from the Cantonal Junta, which body became a prey to internal dissensions. One of its members was assassinated. Taking advantage of these embarrassments of the besieged the republican troops redoubled their efforts. Señor Castelar came down from Madrid to assume the supreme command, and Martinez Campos was superseded by General Lopez Dominguez. An incessant bombardment was kept up, the besieged responding shell by shell. In January the frigate *Tetuan* was burnt to the water's edge, and a day or two later the explosion of the magazine destroyed hundreds of the garrison. The end was near. The city had for half a year defied almost the whole kingdom and withstood the covert attacks of foreign Powers. The Government troops forced their way into wretched, blood-drenched Carthagena; Galvez, Contreras, and the leaders of the cantonal movement escaped by sea in the ironclad *Numancia*, which far exceeded the Government vessels in speed, and took refuge in Algeria. Thus collapsed a movement which was, after the Commune of Paris, the most determined organised attempt ever made to subvert the existing constitution of European society.

I have given at some length this chapter in the history of Carthagena, partly because the town has little interest of itself, and partly because these events though so recent and significant are ignored by most writers of travel books. Out of so much evil good came at last, for these well-nigh fatal disorders opened the eyes of the Spaniards to the instability of the Madrid Government and formed the prelude to the reign of peace inaugurated by the accession to the throne of King Alfonso XII.

Boasting less than most Spanish provinces of sights that appeal only to the casual tourist, Murcia is interesting as a region of perpetual struggle and bloodshed; of struggle against nature, of struggles between differing religions, and of the deadly internecine feuds of race and race.

PLATE 1

VALENCIA: GENERAL VIEW

PLATE 2

VALENCIA: GENERAL VIEW, LOOKING SOUTH

PLATE 3

VALENCIA: VIEW FROM THE PUENTE DEL MAR

PLATE 4

VALENCIA: GENERAL VIEW

PLATE 5

VALENCIA: VIEW FROM THE PUENTE DEL MAR

PLATE 6

VALENCIA: ENTRANCE TO THE TOWN BY THE PUERTA DE SANTA LUCIA

PLATE 7

VALENCIA: THE FAIR AT THE PUERTA DE SANTA LUCIA

Plate 8

VALENCIA: PUERTA DE SERRANOS

PLATE 9

VALENCIA: PUERTA DE CUARTE

PLATE 10

VALENCIA: THE MARKET-PLACE

PLATE 11

VALENCIA: THE PUENTE REAL

PLATE 12

VALENCIA: PASEO DE LA GLORIETA

PLATE 13

VALENCIA: PASEO DE LA GLORIETA

PLATE 14

VALENCIA: PASEO DE LA ALAMEDA

PLATE 15

VALENCIA: FOUNTAIN OF THE ALAMEDA

PLATE 16

VALENCIA: PLAZA DE LA ADUANA

Plate 17

VALENCIA: PLAZA DE SANTO DOMINGO

Plate 18

VALENCIA: PLAZA DE SAN FRANCISCO

PLATE 19

VALENCIA: PLAZA DE TÉTUAN

PLATE 20

VALENCIA: PLAZA DE LA CONSTITUCION

PLATE 21

VALENCIA: CALLE DE LA BAJADA DE SAN FRANCISCO

PLATE 22

VALENCIA: CALLE DE SAN VICENTE

PLATE 23

VALENCIA: TROS ALT

PLATE 24

VALENCIA: CALLE DE LA BOLSERIA Y TROS ALT

PLATE 25

VALENCIA: GENERAL VIEW OF THE CATHEDRAL

PLATE 26

VALENCIA CATHEDRAL: GATE OF THE APOSTLES

PLATE 27

VALENCIA: THE CATHEDRAL, PUERTA DEL PALAU

PLATE 28

VALENCIA CATHEDRAL: A DOOR

PLATE 29

VALENCIA: THE TEMPLE

PLATE 30

VALENCIA: THE MIGUELETE

PLATE 31

VALENCIA: CHURCH OF SANTA CATALINA

PLATE 32

VALENCIA: CHURCH OF SANTA CATALINA

PLATE 33

VALENCIA: CHURCH OF LOS SANTOS JUANES

VALENCIA: FAÇADE OF SAN MIGUEL EL REAL

PLATE 35

VALENCIA: CHURCH OF SANTA CRUZ

PLATE 36

VALENCIA: CHURCH OF SANTA CRUZ

PLATE 37

VALENCIA: ENTRANCE TO THE CHURCH OF SAN ANDRÉS

PLATE 38

VALENCIA: THE CAMPO-SANTO

PLATE 39

VALENCIA: THE CAMPO-SANTO

PLATE 40

VALENCIA: THE CAMPO-SANTO

PLATE 41

VALENCIA: THE AUDIENCIA, OLD PALACE OF THE CORTES

PLATE 42

VALENCIA: ROYAL HALL IN THE AUDIENCIA, UPPER PART

PLATE 43

VALENCIA: ROYAL HALL IN THE AUDIENCIA, LOWER PART

PLATE 44

VALENCIA: INTERIOR DOOR OF THE AUDIENCIA

PLATE 45

VALENCIA: THE EXCHANGE

PLATE 46

VALENCIA: THE EXCHANGE. DETAIL OF THE GALLERY

PLATE 47

VALENCIA: INTERIOR OF THE EXCHANGE

PLATE 48

VALENCIA: INTERIOR DOOR OF THE EXCHANGE

PLATE 49

VALENCIA: COLEGIO DEL PATRIARCA

PLATE 50

VALENCIA: COURTYARD IN THE COLEGIO DEL PATRIARCA

Plate 51

VALENCIA: COURTYARD OF THE UNIVERSITY

Plate 52

VALENCIA: ENTRANCE TO THE CIVIL HOSPITAL

VALENCIA: GATE OF MOSEN S'ORRELL

PLATE 54

VALENCIA: THE CUSTOM-HOUSE

PLATE 55

VALENCIA: THE ARCHBISHOP'S PALACE

PLATE 56

VALENCIA: THE BULL-RING

PLATE 57

VALENCIA: TOBACCO FACTORY

PLATE 58

VALENCIA: A PRIVATE HOUSE

PLATE 59

VALENCIA: STATUE OF KING JAIME

PLATE 60

VALENCIA: STATUE OF RIBERA

VALENCIA: STATUE OF ST. CHRISTOPHER

PLATE 62

VALENCIA: PALACE OF THE MARQUÉS DE DOS AGUAS

PLATE 63

VALENCIA: PALACE OF THE MARQUÉS DE DOS AGUAS

VALENCIA: PORTAL OF THE PALACE OF THE MARQUÉS DE DOS AGUAS

PLATE 65

VALENCIA: PALACE OF THE MARQUES DE RIPALDA

PLATE 66

GENERAL VIEW OF GRAO

PLATE 67

GRAO HARBOUR

PLATE 68

GRAO HARBOUR

PLATE 69

GRAO HARBOUR

PLATE 70

CAMINO DEL GRAO: HERMITAGE OF AVE MARIA

PLATE 71

VALENCIA: A "TARTANA," OR CHAR-À-BANC

PLATE 72

VALENCIA: PEASANTS

PLATE 73

VALENCIA: PEASANTS

PLATE 74

VALENCIA: PEASANTS

PLATE 75

VALENCIA: TYPES OF WOMEN

PLATE 76

VALENCIA: TRIBUNAL DES EAUX

PLATE 77

VALENCIA: BARBERS ON THE BRIDGE OF SERRANOS

PLATE 78

VALENCIA: ZIGZAG OF THE CABRILLAS

PLATE 79

ENVIRONS OF VALENCIA: A ROAD IN CABAÑAL

PLATE 80

ENVIRONS OF VALENCIA: A ROAD IN CABAÑAL

PLATE 81

VALENCIA: THE SHORES OF THE MEDITERRANEAN

PLATE 82

VALENCIA: THE SHORES OF THE MEDITERRANEAN

PLATE 83

MURVIEDRO: GENERAL VIEW

PLATE 84

MURVIEDRO: GENERAL VIEW

PLATE 85

MURVIEDRO: VIEW FROM THE STATION

PLATE 86

MURVIEDRO: VIEW FROM THE CASTLE

PLATE 87

MURVIEDRO: THE CASTLE AND TOWN

PLATE 88

MURVIEDRO: THE CASTLE

PLATE 89

MURVIEDRO: THE CASTLE FROM ONE OF THE COURTS

PLATE 90

MURVIEDRO: ENTRANCE TO THE CASTLE

PLATE 91

MURVIEDRO: GENERAL VIEW OF THE ROMAN
AMPHITHEATRE

PLATE 92

MURVIEDRO: GENERAL VIEW OF THE ROMAN
AMPHITHEATRE

PLATE 93

MURVIEDRO: THE ROMAN AMPHITHEATRE

PLATE 94

MURVIEDRO: INTERIOR OF THE ROMAN AMPHITHEATRE

PLATE 95

MURVIEDRO: PRINCIPAL GATE OF THE ROMAN AMPHITHEATRE

PLATE 96

MURVIEDRO: ENTRANCE TO THE ROMAN AMPHITHEATRE

PLATE 97

MURVIEDRO: ENTRANCE TO THE ROMAN AMPHITHEATRE

PLATE 98

JATIVA: GENERAL VIEW

PLATE 99

JATIVA: VIEW FROM THE STATION

PLATE 100

JATIVA: THE CIVIL HOSPITAL

PLATE 101

ALICANTE: GENERAL VIEW

PLATE 102

ALICANTE: THE CASTLE

PLATE 103

ALICANTE: VIEW FROM THE CASTLE

PLATE 104

ALICANTE: THE BREAKWATER

PLATE 105

ALICANTE: GENERAL VIEW

PLATE 106

ALICANTE: GENERAL VIEW

PLATE 107

ALICANTE: GENERAL VIEW

PLATE 108

ALICANTE: PASEO DE LOS MARTIRES

PLATE 109

ALICANTE: PASEO DE LOS MARTIRES

PLATE 110

ALICANTE: PASEO DE LOS MARTIRES

PLATE 111

ALICANTE: PASEO DE LOS MARTIRES

PLATE 112

ALICANTE: PASEO DE NUÑEZ

PLATE 113

ALICANTE: THE TOWN HALL

PLATE 114

ALICANTE: THE TOWN HALL

PLATE 115

ALICANTE: MONUMENT TO QUIJANO

PLATE 116

ALICANTE: THE BULL-RING

PLATE 117

ELCHE: GENERAL VIEW

PLATE 118

ELCHE: GENERAL VIEW

PLATE 119

ELCHE: GENERAL VIEW

PLATE 120

ELCHE: VIEW OF THE TOWN

PLATE 121

ELCHE: PLAZA MAYOR

PLATE 122

ELCHE: VIEW FROM THE STATION

PLATE 123

ELCHE: THE ROAD TO ALICANTE

PLATE 124

ELCHE: THE ROAD FROM ALICANTE

PLATE 125

ELCHE: THE TOWN HALL

PLATE 126

ELCHE: CHURCH OF SAN JUAN

PLATE 127

ELCHE: BRIDGE OVER THE RAMBLA DE ELCHE

PLATE 128

ELCHE: VIEW FROM THE RAILWAY BRIDGE

PLATE 129

ELCHE: THE CANAL

PLATE 130

ELCHE: WASHING LINEN IN THE CANAL

PLATE 131

ELCHE: A CANAL

PLATE 132

ELCHE: TOWER OF RAPSAMBLANC, BELONGING TO THE CONDE DE LUNA

PLATE 133

ELCHE: CASTLE OF THE DUQUE DE ALTAMIRA, NOW A PRISON

PLATE 134

ELCHE: MILL AND CASTLE OF THE DUQUE DE ALTAMIRA

PLATE 135

ELCHE: CASTLE OF THE DUQUE DE ALTAMIRA

PLATE 136

ELCHE: CASTLE AND MILL

PLATE 137

ELCHE: PALMS

PLATE 138

ELCHE: COUNTRY SPINNERS

PLATE 139

ELCHE: CASA DE LA HUERTA

PLATE 140

ELCHE: A COUNTRY ROAD

PLATE 141

ELCHE: A COUNTRY HOUSE

PLATE 142

ELCHE: A COUNTRY HOUSE

PLATE 143

ELCHE: A FAMOUS PALM

PLATE 144

ELCHE: A PALM CELEBRATED FOR ITS RESEMBLANCE TO A COLUMN

PLATE 145

ELCHE: PALM GROVES

PLATE 146

ELCHE: A ROAD

PLATE 147

SAX: GENERAL VIEW

PLATE 148

MURCIA: GENERAL VIEW

PLATE 149

MURCIA: VIEW FROM THE TOWER OF THE CATHEDRAL,
TOWARDS THE SOUTH

PLATE 150

MURCIA: VIEW OF THE TOWN

PLATE 151

MURCIA: GENERAL VIEW OF THE TOWN

PLATE 152

MURCIA: GENERAL VIEW OF THE TOWN

PLATE 153

MURCIA: GENERAL VIEW OF THE TOWN

PLATE 154

MURCIA: GENERAL VIEW

PLATE 155

MURCIA: THE BRIDGE

PLATE 156

MURCIA: THE RIVER

PLATE 157

MURCIA: THE BRIDGE OVER THE SEGURA

PLATE 158

MURCIA: THE RIVER SEGURA

PLATE 159

MURCIA: THE FAIR

PLATE 160

MURCIA: THE FAIR

PLATE 161

MURCIA: THE MARKET-PLACE

PLATE 162

MURCIA: PLAZA DE SANTO DOMINGO ON MARKET-DAY

PLATE 163

MURCIA: PASEO DEL MALECON

PLATE 164

MURCIA: PLAZA DE SANTA CATALINA

PLATE 165

MURCIA: PLAZA DE TOROS, NOW PLAZA DE SAN AUGUSTIN

PLATE 166

MURCIA: PASEO DEL ARENAL

PLATE 167

MURCIA: PLAZA DE SAN PEDRO

PLATE 168

MURCIA: PASEO DE FLORIDABLANCA AND PALACE OF THE EXHIBITION

PLATE 169

MURCIA: PLAZA DE SANTA ISABELLA

PLATE 170

MURCIA: CALLE DEL PUENTE

PLATE 171

MURCIA: PLAZA DE LA GLORIÉTA

PLATE 172

MURCIA: PLAZA DE LA GLORIÉTA

PLATE 173

MURCIA: THE CATHEDRAL

PLATE 174

MURCIA: GENERAL VIEW OF THE CATHEDRAL

PLATE 175

MURCIA: PRINCIPAL FAÇADE OF THE CATHEDRAL

PLATE 176

MURCIA: TOWER OF THE CATHEDRAL

PLATE 177

MURCIA: SIDE DOOR OF THE CATHEDRAL

PLATE 178

MURCIA CATHEDRAL: GATE OF THE APOSTLES

MURCIA CATHEDRAL: CHAPEL OF THE MARQUÉS DE LOS VELEZ

MURCIA CATHEDRAL: DETAIL OF THE FAÇADE

PLATE 181

MURCIA: DETAIL OF THE CATHEDRAL

PLATE 182

MURCIA CATHEDRAL: WINDOW OF THE BELFRY

PLATE 183

MURCIA CATHEDRAL: PRINCIPAL NAVE

PLATE 184

MURCIA CATHEDRAL: LATERAL NAVE

PLATE 185

MURCIA CATHEDRAL: BEHIND THE CHOIR

PLATE 186

MURCIA CATHEDRAL: ENTRANCE TO THE CHAPEL OF THE
MARQUÉS DE LOS VELEZ

MURCIA CATHEDRAL: CHAPEL OF THE MARQUÉS DE LOS VELEZ

MURCIA CATHEDRAL: THE HIGH ALTAR

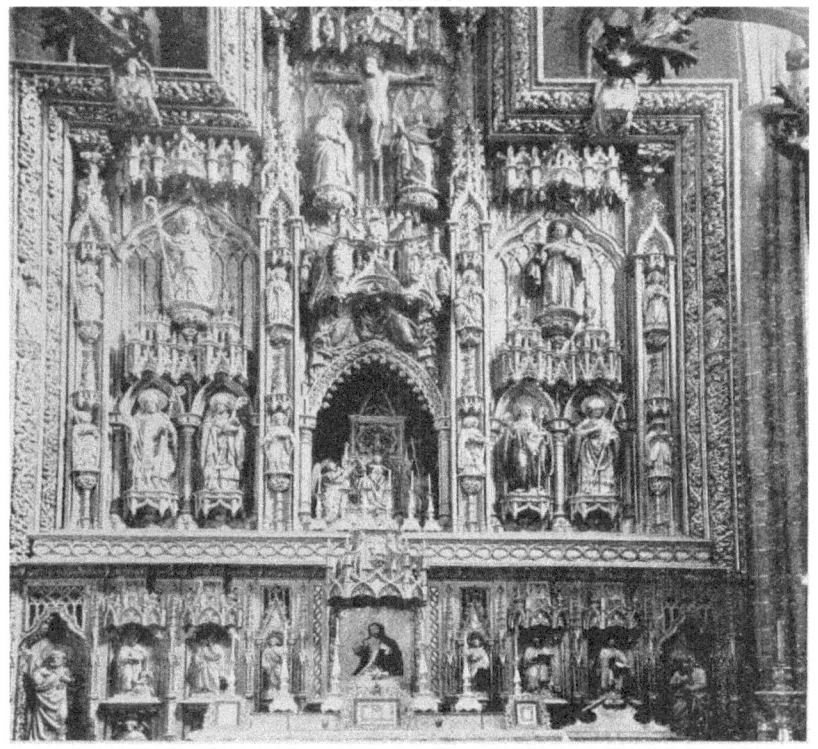

MURCIA CATHEDRAL: THE HIGH ALTAR

PLATE 190

MURCIA CATHEDRAL: GENERAL VIEW OF THE CHOIR

PLATE 191

MURCIA CATHEDRAL: THE BISHOP'S THRONE, IN THE CHOIR

MURCIA CATHEDRAL: DETAIL OF THE CHOIR STALLS

PLATE 193

MURCIA CATHEDRAL: DETAIL OF THE CHOIR STALLS

PLATE 194

MURCIA CATHEDRAL: THE SACRISTY

PLATE 195

MURCIA CATHEDRAL: TOMB OF ALFONSO THE WISE

MURCIA: CHURCH OF SANTO DOMINGO

MURCIA: CHURCH OF SANTO DOMINGO

PLATE 198

MURCIA: CHURCH OF SAN BARTOLOMÉ

PLATE 199

MURCIA: FAÇADE OF THE CONVENT DE LA MISERICORDIA

Plate 200

MURCIA: PALACE OF THE MARQUÉS DE VILLAFRANCA DE LOS VELEZ AND CONVENT OF SANTA CLARA

Plate 201

MURCIA: THE EPISCOPAL PALACE

PLATE 202

MURCIA: CASA HUERTA DE LAS BOMBAS

MURCIA: PALACE OF THE MARQUÉS DE ALMODOVAR

PLATE 204

MURCIA: PALACE OF THE BARON DE ALBALA

PLATE 205

MURCIA: PALACE OF THE MARQUÉS DE ESPINARDO

PLATE 206

MURCIA: THE "CONTRASTE"

PLATE 207

MURCIA: MONUMENT TO SALZILLO

PLATE 208

MURCIA: ROMAN ALTAR DEDICATED TO PEACE, FOUND IN CARTHAGENA AND MOVED IN 1594 TO THE PALACE OF THE MARQUÉS DE ESPINARDO

Plate 209

MURCIA: HOUSE IN THE CALLE JABONERIA

PLATE 210

MURCIA: HOUSE OF THE PAINTER VILLASIS

PLATE 211

MURCIA: A BALCONY IN THE CALLE TRAPERIA

PLATE 212

MURCIA: PUERTA CADENAS

PLATE 213

MURCIA: TEATRO DE ROMEA

PLATE 214

MURCIA: THE BULL RING

PLATE 215

MURCIA: THE TOWN HALL

PLATE 216

MURCIA: THE TOWN HALL

PLATE 217

MURCIA: PROCESSION LEAVING THE CHURCH OF JESUS IN
HOLY WEEK ST. VERONICA

PLATE 218

PROCESSION LEAVING THE CHURCH OF JESUS IN HOLY
WEEK—THE KISS OF JUDAS

PLATE 219

MURCIA: PROCESSION IN HOLY WEEK. THE GARDEN OF
GETHSEMANE

PLATE 220

MURCIA: PROCESSION IN HOLY WEEK. OUR LORD FALLING

PLATE 221

MURCIA: PROCESSION IN HOLY WEEK. THE SCOURGING

PLATE 222

MURCIA: CHURCH OF JESUS THE LAST SUPPER, BY ZARZILLO

PLATE 223

MURCIA: PILGRIMAGE OF ST. BLAS

PLATE 224

MURCIA: RUINS OF THE ARAB BATHS

PLATE 225

ENVIRONS OF MURCIA: CONVENT OF SAN JERONIMO

PLATE 226

ENVIRONS OF MURCIA: HERMITAGE OF THE FUENSANTA

PLATE 227

ENVIRONS OF MURCIA: HERMITAGE OF THE FUENSANTA

PLATE 228

ENVIRONS OF MURCIA: HERMITAGE OF THE FUENSANTA

PLATE 229

ENVIRONS OF MURCIA: CASTLE OF MONTEAGUDO

PLATE 230

MURCIA: PAISAJE DE LA HUERTA

PLATE 231

MURCIA: PAISAJE DE LA HUERTA

PLATE 232

MURCIA: PAISAJE DE LA HUERTA

PLATE 233

MURCIA: A CART LOADED WITH "TINAJAS"

PLATE 234

MURCIA: HARVEST-TIME

PLATE 235

ENVIRONS OF MURCIA: THE HUERTA DES CAPUCINS

PLATE 236

ENVIRONS OF MURCIA: THE HUERTA DES CAPUCINS

PLATE 237

ENVIRONS OF MURCIA: VIEW FROM THE HUERTA DES CAPUCINS

PLATE 238

ENVIRONS OF MURCIA: THE HUERTA DES CAPUCINS, DATE-GATHERING

PLATE 239

ORIHUELA: GENERAL VIEW

PLATE 240

ORIHUELA: GENERAL VIEW FROM THE PUERTA DE MURCIA

PLATE 241

ORIHUELA: THE RIVER SEGURA

PLATE 242

ORIHUELA: THE RIVER SEGURA FROM THE EAST

ORIHUELA: DOOR OF THE CHURCH OF SANTIAGO

PLATE 244

CARTHAGENA: GENERAL VIEW

PLATE 245

CARTHAGENA: A PARTIAL VIEW.

Plate 246

CARTHAGENA: VIEW FROM THE STATION

Plate 247

CARTHAGENA: VIEW FROM THE HIGH ROAD

PLATE 248

CARTHAGENA: VIEW FROM QUITAPELLIJOS

PLATE 249

CARTHAGENA: VIEW FROM THE FORT OF ATALAYA

PLATE 250

CARTHAGENA: VIEW FROM THE FORT OF ATALAYA

PLATE 251

CARTHAGENA: VIEW FROM ST. JOSEPH'S MILL

PLATE 252

CARTHAGENA: VIEW FROM ST. JOSEPH'S MILL

PLATE 253

CARTHAGENA: VIEW FROM THE FORT OF GALERA

PLATE 254

CARTHAGENA: VIEW FROM THE FORT OF GALERA

PLATE 255

CARTHAGENA: VIEW OF THE HARBOUR

PLATE 256

CARTHAGENA: SANTA LUCIA AND THE HARBOUR

PLATE 257

CARTHAGENA: THE HARBOUR FROM SANTA LUCIA

PLATE 258

CARTHAGENA: THE HARBOUR FROM SANTA LUCIA

PLATE 259

CARTHAGENA: THE HARBOUR FROM THE POWDER MAGAZINE

PLATE 260

CARTHAGENA: THE HARBOUR FROM TRINCABATIJOS

PLATE 261

CARTHAGENA: VIEW FROM THE ESPLANADERO

PLATE 262

CARTHAGENA: THE ENTRANCE TO THE HARBOUR FROM TRINCABATIJOS

PLATE 263

CARTHAGENA: THE BREAKWATER

PLATE 264

CARTHAGENA: ENTRANCE TO THE HARBOUR

PLATE 265

CARTHAGENA: ENTRANCE TO THE ARSENAL

PLATE 266

CARTHAGENA: PUERTA DEL MAR

PLATE 267

CARTHAGENA: PUERTA DE MURCIA

PLATE 268

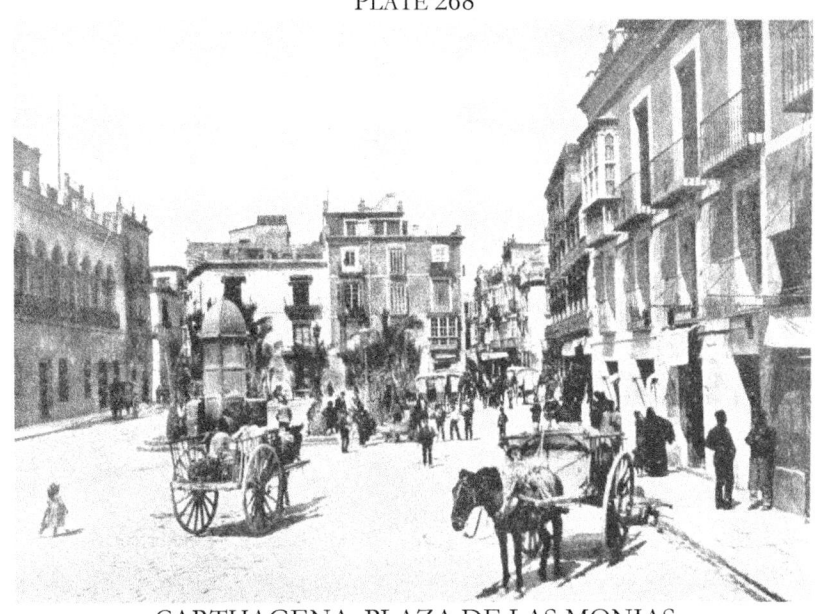

CARTHAGENA: PLAZA DE LAS MONJAS

PLATE 269

CARTHAGENA: THE MARINE COLLEGE

PLATE 270

CARTHAGENA: THE BULL-RING

PLATE 271

ARCHENA: THE BATHS, FROM LA SIERRA DE VERDELENA

PLATE 272

ARCHENA: GENERAL VIEW OF THE BATHS FROM THE WEST

PLATE 273

ARCHENA: GENERAL VIEW OF THE BATHS AT THE
ENTRANCE TO THE VILLAGE

PLATE 274

ARCHENA: ENTRANCE TO THE BATHS

PLATE 275

ARCHENA: THE CARRETERA AND RIVER SEGURA

PLATE 276

ARCHENA: VIEW OF THE CHURCH

PLATE 277

ARCHENA: INTERIOR OF THE CHURCH

PLATE 278

ARCHENA: THE CHURCH: ALTAR OF THE "VIRGEN DE LA SALUD"

PLATE 279

ENVIRONS OF ARCHENA: VIEW OF VILLANUEVA

PLATE 280

ENVIRONS OF ARCHENA: VIEW OF BLANCA FROM THE SALTO DEL PALOMO

PLATE 281

ENVIRONS OF ARCHENA: VIEW OF BLANCA FROM BUJAMENTE

PLATE 282

ENVIRONS OF ARCHENA: VILLAGE AND GARDENS OF ULEA FROM VILLANUEVA

PLATE 283

ENVIRONS OF ARCHENA: VILLAGE AND GARDENS OF ULEA, EAST SIDE

PLATE 284

ENVIRONS OF ARCHENA: VILLAGE OF OJOS AND MOUNTAINS

PLATE 285

ENVIRONS OF ARCHENA: THE GARDENS OF OJOS, FROM THE LOVERS' LEAP

PLATE 286

ENVIRONS OF ARCHENA: THE LOVERS' LEAP

PLATE 287

LORCA: GENERAL VIEW

PLATE 288

LORCA: VIEW FROM THE RAILWAY STATION